CREATE ·

DANCE OF THE HANDS

Channeled by Rae Chandran
with Robert Mason Pollock

Other Books by Rae Chandran with Robert Mason Pollock

DNA of the Spirit, Volume 1

DNA of the Spirit, Volume 2

Partner with Angels

Coming Soon

The Universal Codes of Creation

DANCE OF THE
HANDS

CREATE · MANIFEST · HEAL

Channeled by Rae Chandran
with Robert Mason Pollock

3 LIGHT
Technology
PUBLISHING

For more information about special discounts for bulk purchases, please contact Light Technology Publishing Special Sales at 1-800-450-0985 or publishing@LightTechnology.net.

Also available as an e-book from your favorite e-book distributor.

ISBN-13: 978-1-62233-038-6

Published and printed in the United States of America by

PO Box 3540
Flagstaff, AZ 86003
1-800-450-0985 or 928-526-1345
www.LightTechnology.com

Contents

Dance of the Hands is dedicated to

All That Is

and All That Was

and All That Ever Will Be.

Foreword

Rae Chandran has been teaching workshops on mudras for a number of years, so it is only natural that a book would evolve from all the material he has been given. The number of practices has more than doubled since the true scope of this book became apparent.

I traveled with Rae to three countries in the eastern Mediterranean. Some practices came through on a hotel patio on the banks of the Nile, and others were channeled on a bus on the highways of Greece. The final series in this book was received in an apartment in Great Barrington, Massachusetts. More mudras will follow in a second book on partnering with angels, and these will be combined with breathing techniques and sound.

Some of these mudras have sounds; others do not. Some are static; others have movement. Some are for healing Earth; others are for children or for ascension. I taught several workshops using this material, and I found that an effective way of presenting these mudras was to not tell the participants the name of what they were practicing. That way, they had to feel the energies with their bodies, allowing their minds to take a back seat.

Many people helped bring this book into being. Amanda Sewell, Ari Greenberg, and Kevin Diamond all appear in the photographs (all of which I took), along with some people from the tour Rae led who appear on a beach in Naxos, Greece. Kevin Diamond and Christine St. Clare helped me organize the material.

Robert Pollock
Pittsfield, Massachusetts
June 2015

Preface

Making *The Dance of the Hands* has been a collaborative effort. The material was channeled from many inner masters like Archangel Metatron, Archangel Michael, Master Serapis Bey, Master Thoth, Gaia, Cleopatra, and King Akhenaton.

Using the body to create energies was taught by the ancient ones who visited this planet from other star systems and galaxies. This material originates from the ancient practices of the Maya, Pharaonic Egyptians, and the people of the Indus Valley civilizations. These ancient ones understood using the body to create specific energies, and they used these techniques to heal many physical ailments, as well as the emotional and mental bodies.

Healing a specific part of the body is based on the principles of quantum healing. Full-body healing takes place when one part of the body is fully healed. Holding the fingers in certain positions generates energy, and through the innate wisdom of the body, this generated energy is sent to the afflicted parts of the body to bring about healing.

Holding the fingers in certain positions to create energy is very simple. The thumb represents the energy or the wisdom of the I Am presence, and the index finger represents the personality and the mind. When the power of the thumb presses against the index finger, the higher energy from the thumb is pushed into the index finger and the mind. This energy then circulates through the palms of the hand and activates the healing chakra, which is in the middle of the palm. The energy then flows to the afflicted parts of the body to bring about healing. These techniques can be further enhanced when they are combined with breathing and sound. They then become very powerful, transformative, and healing tools.

I hope that you get as much out of this work as I have.

Rae Chandran
Tokyo, Japan
June 2015

How to Use This Book
Archangel Metatron and Archangel Michael
August 5, 2015

This book is for everyone, not just people who are spiritually advanced. It is for any layperson, regardless of religion. This material is for those who have an interest in bettering themselves or improving their well-being — practitioners, teachers, masters, the spiritually advanced, neophytes, and children. It is like yoga. Yoga is not related to any religion, and it is not only for spiritually advanced people. Yoga is for those who want to feel good in their bodies.

The **purpose** of these mudras is simple: to bring balance to the body, mind, and soul. Like any spiritual practice, doing mudras brings balance to every area of your life. The **benefits** are simple as well: These mudras bring joy and peace to your life. There are many other benefits, but the ultimate benefit is coming to a joyful and peaceful state. When you are joyful and peaceful, you are more likely to access the higher aspects of your consciousness.

This material came from many beings, principally Archangel Metatron, Archangel Michael, Thoth, King Akhenaton, Isis, and the higher self of Rae. Why did these beings offer this information? The answer is very simple: It is another tool for the awakening of humanity.

YOUR MUDRA PRACTICE

There are no hard and fast rules about **where** these mudras should be practiced. You can practice hand movements anywhere you want. Indoors, outdoors — anywhere is fine. It is only important to practice where you feel relaxed and comfortable, where you have space to do them, and where you can be silent. That is how to practice them. As for preparation, it is not a question of preparing the space. It is a question of how you prepare yourself to be in a state of relaxation: by getting in touch with your feeling bodies.

These mudras are **best practiced individually** except when they are being taught in a class. There is no set **time** for practicing a mudra, but three minutes is a good benchmark.

How often should you practice? This is an individual choice. If you feel benefit, then continue. **Focus** on your body, the energy movements in your body, and your feelings.

Some mudras are accompanied by sounds and others are not. Using sounds can enhance certain mudra positions. Others do not need sounds to enhance their energy. Some mudras need an extra boost using sound frequency. Others already have high-frequency energy and do not need sound enhancement.

You do not need to be stationary when doing mudras. Children can practice the mudras while dancing and playing. When children play and dance, they are fully present. Adults are rarely completely present. Even when they are dancing and playing, their minds are often on something else. When they are stationary, they are often more relaxed, and they can control their consciousnesses more easily.

Some mudras have as many as five different poses, depending on where the mudra originated. We bring forth the pose that is most suitable for the Earth plane.

There are twelve DNA mudras that correspond with the twelve strands of DNA. These mudras should be done as one set. They are mudras just for DNA. You cannot take one of these and do it on its own. They are done in a set of twelve mudras just for DNA.

As for the other mudras, there is **no order**. The mudras are not presented in any particular order. It is up to each person to choose where to begin. Pick a mudra that resonates with you and begin there. Do it with the full focus of your body, mind, and soul. Be fully invested in it.

Practicing these mudras can bring you **calmness**, a sense of **well-being**, and a heightened sense of **awareness**. Each person will have individual reactions or results. Over time, you will notice a sense of **balance** and **empowerment** coming into your life. Relationships can be healed and reconciled. You will become more tolerant, more accepting, and less judgmental. You will have a sense that you are part of the whole and that you are your brother's/sister's keeper. The mudras for healing Earth obviously have global results.

RECOMMENDATIONS

These mudras are tools from the ancient past. They have been used by many generations of people to bring about healing, well-being, serenity, and peace. To use any tool well, you need to **practice** using it. You will surely see a difference in the energy around you, in your aura, in your chi, and in your mental perception. To master anything, you must practice. Our suggestion is simple: practice, practice, practice.

This book will help you connect the dots. There is much truth available. This book is one dot. There are many dots to be connected to attain liberation and enlightenment. We do not want to say that ours is the only truth. It is just one dot in the whole.

Healing and Growth

Deep Appreciation

Hands are in prayer position pointing upward.

Deep Gratitude

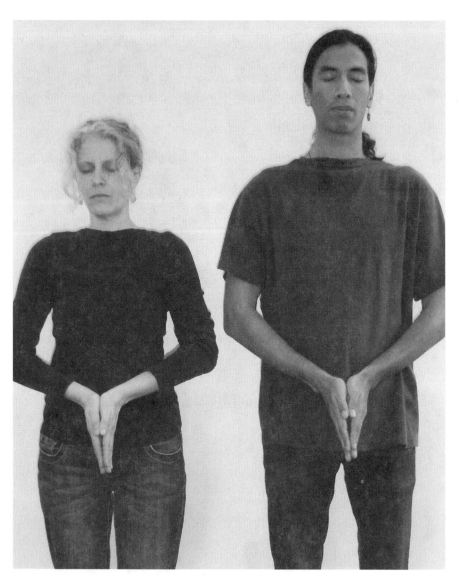

Hands are in prayer position pointing downward.

Balance in Giving and Receiving

*Both thumbs and ring fingers touch, and
the right wrist is on top of the left wrist.*

Balance in Love Relationships

Both thumbs and index fingers touch.
Both wrists touch, and the palms are open horizontally.

Unity of Body, Mind, and Soul

Both thumbs and index fingers touch to make circles.
The left circle is inside the right circle but not touching.

Unity of Body and Mind

*Both thumbs and middle fingers touch to make circles.
The left circle is inside the right but not touching.*

Unity of Body and Soul

Both thumbs and ring fingers touch to make circles.
The left circle is inside the right circle but not touching.

Connection with the Elements
(Earth, Wind, Water, and Fire)

Both thumbs and pinky fingers touch to make circles.
The left circle is inside the right circle but not touching.

Friendship with Oneself

The right index finger is extended inside the left fist.
Both are vertical.

Friendship from the Heart

*I. Both fists are closed with the knuckles touching
and elbows out horizontally.*

*II. Both hands are open and touching the heart
with the right hand higher than the left.*

Compassion from the Heart

*The right hand is placed over the heart with the thumb
and pinky finger touching and other fingers extended.*

Truthfulness from the Heart

*Both thumbs are under the middle and ring fingers.
The hands are placed over the heart with the
right hand higher than the left.*

Knowledge and Wisdom

Both thumbs and index fingers touch and are placed horizontally over the solar plexus. The circles made by the thumbs and index fingers should face outward.

Center

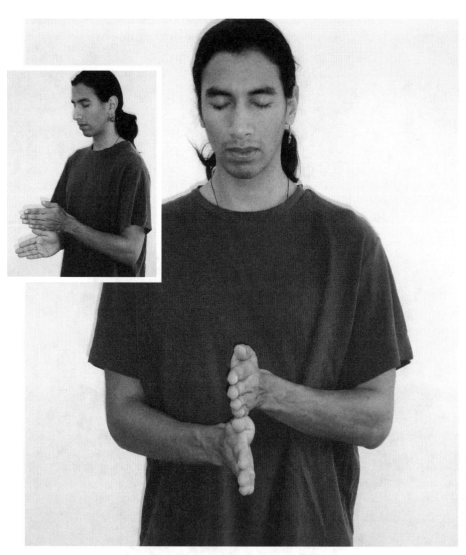

The fingers of the left hand are extended but touching and pointing away from the body. The right hand is in a similar position underneath the left hand. The left pinky lies on top of the right thumb, and the fingers create a vertical stack. The hands should be perpendicular to the body.

Heartfelt Communication

Both thumbs and pinky fingers touch, and both hands are held horizontally in front of the heart chakra.

Release

Both palms are open. The backs of both hands face each other (but do not touch). The left hand is over the right, and the wrists touch to make an X, fingertips pointing away from the body.

Boost Energy to Complete a Task

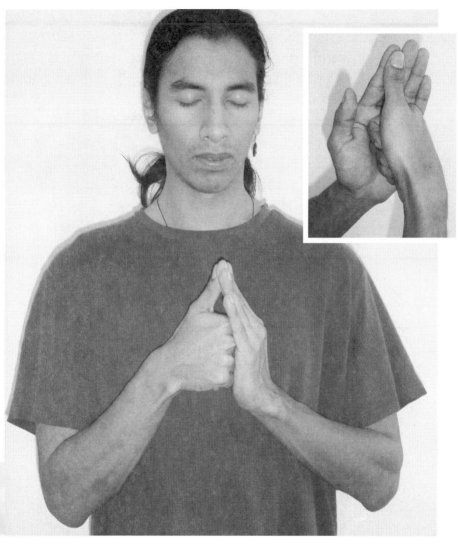

The fingers of the left hand are extended fully while the fingers of the right hand are closed. The right thumb is open and presses strongly on the tip of the left index finger. The right fist touches the left palm, and both hands are held in front of the chest.

Reconnection

Both thumbs and index fingers touch and are placed on top of the shoulders with the elbows out to the sides.

Balance between Male and Female Polarities

The right hand is slightly cupped, and the arm is extended forward. The left hand is open, and the arm is bent. Both palms face away from the heart.

Divinity

I. Both palms are open, facing downward, and raised over the head, fingertips pointing toward each other.

II. Slowly bring both hands down in front of the heart chakra with middle fingers touching.

Calm Anxiety and Fear

Both thumbs and pinky fingers touch and are held palm-up in front of the heart chakra, pinkies and thumbs closest to the body.

Yin and Yang
(or Absolute and Relative)

Both thumbs and index fingers touch and are held in front of the heart chakra (palms toward each other, fingertips upward), left hand slightly above the right.

Be Open to Higher Truths

Both thumbs and ring fingers touch and are held horizontally in front of the heart chakra (palms up).

Truthful Communication from Source
(or Communication with Feeling and Understanding from Source)

The fingers of both hands are fully open and spread apart. The fingertips of both hands touch each other. The tips of the thumbs touch and are pointed to the navel. The body cannot lie in this position.
Sound: oooommmm

Harmony

Balance on left leg with right leg bent back, the heel as close to the buttocks as possible. Touch both palms together over the head.

Activate the Angel Chakra

*I. Hold both hands in prayer position
in the center of the chest.*

II. Slowly raise hands to forehead above the third eye.

I Feel Worthy

The right thumb, index finger, and middle finger are open and point upward. The other two fingers are closed.
Sound: iiii yummmm

Calm Emotions

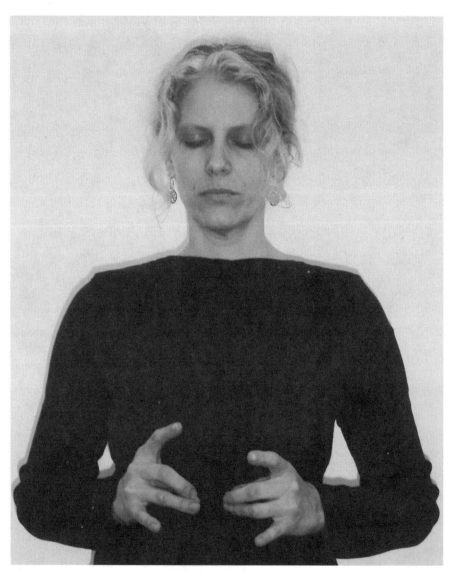

Both thumbs touch the middle and ring fingers and are held horizontally (palms facing the body) over the solar plexus.

Calm Panic

Both thumbs touch the pinky fingers and are held horizontally over the solar plexus. The other fingers are pointed away from the body.

The Law of One

Both hands are closed into fists and touch each other over the heart. The right index finger is raised and points away from the body.

Heaven and Earth

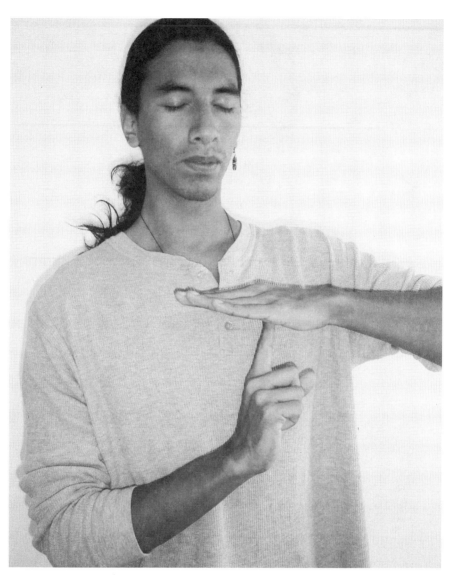

The left hand is completely open and is held horizontally (palm down) in front of the heart. The right index finger points upward and touches the middle of the left palm.

Ascension

*Both thumbs, index fingers, and pinky fingers are open
and touch each other with hands held in front of the
heart. The other fingers on each hand are closed.
Sound: aaaa maaaay aaaa ommmm*

Courage

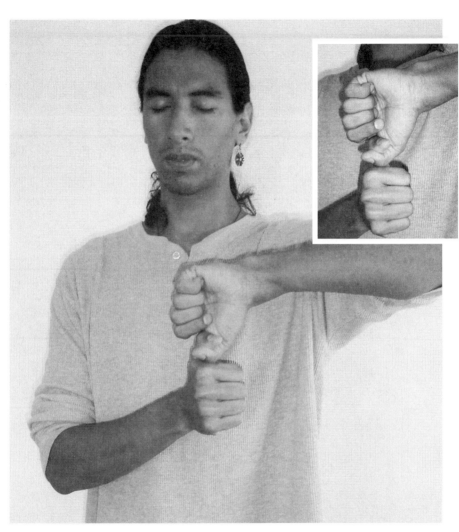

Both hands make fists. The left fist (palm forward, away from body) is over the right fist (palm toward body), stacked vertically. The right thumb is hooked over the left thumb. Bring hands in front of the heart and breathe to the hands. Imagine that you are breathing into an infinity loop.

Trust

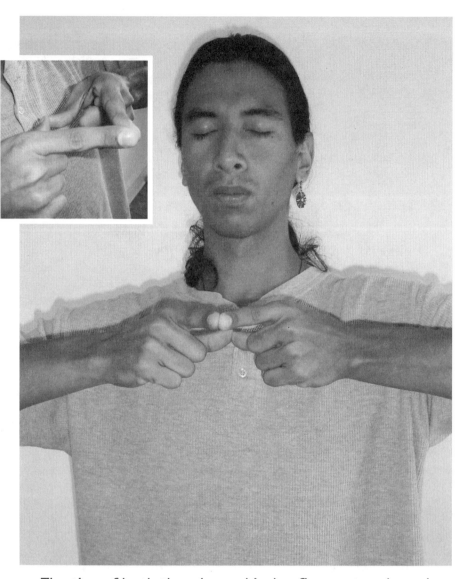

The tips of both thumbs and index fingers touch each other. Both hands' middle, ring, and pinky fingers are closed. You should see a big triangle when you look down. Bring your hands between your heart and throat chakras.

Faith

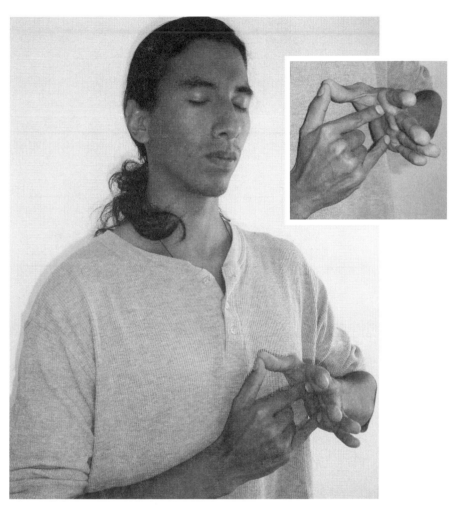

Both thumbs touch each other. The index and pinky fingers of the right hand are extended while the middle and ring fingers are down and touch the palm. The right hand's index and pinky fingers press into the palm of the open left hand. The left hand is a little higher than the right hand. Hold both hands between the heart and solar plexus. The left fingers point away from the body.

Hope

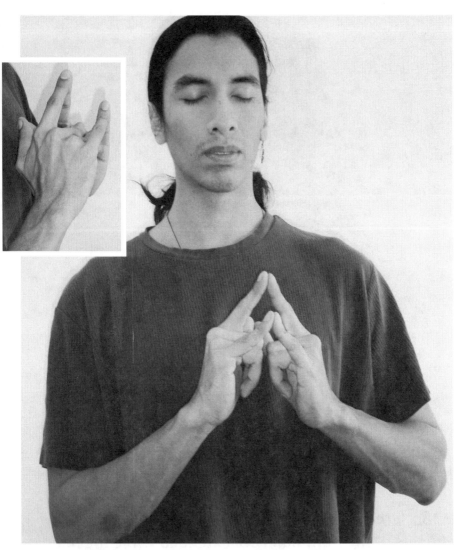

The tips of both thumbs, index fingers, and pinky fingers touch each other. The middle and ring fingers are closed. Place both hands in front of the heart and breathe through the gap created by the not-extended middle and ring fingers.

Relieve Challenging Energy in Your Daily Life

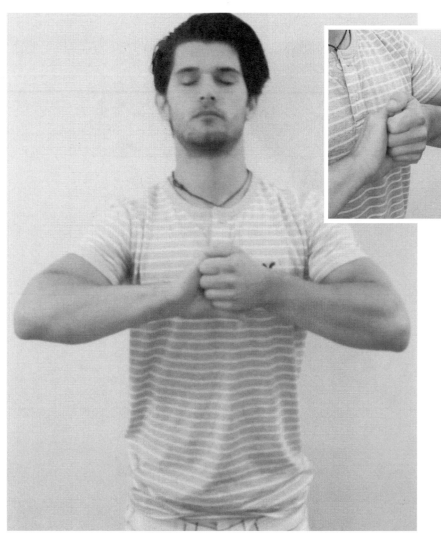

The fingers of both hands are curled so that the hands interlock with each other horizontally and are held in front of the upper chest. The right palm faces toward the body, and the left faces away.

Bring in Energies
of the Higher Chakras
(Up to Ten)

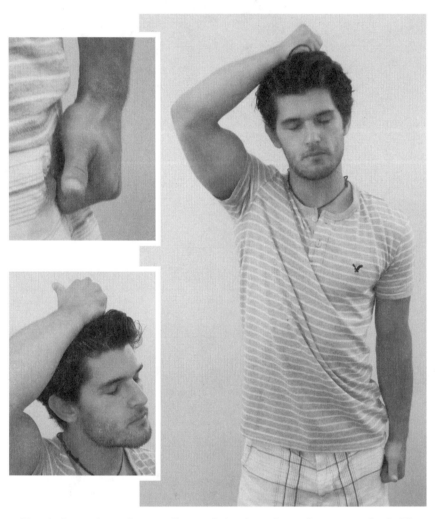

Each hand makes a fist with the thumb extended. The right hand is held at the crown chakra with the thumb pointing upward. The left hand is down at the side of the body with the elbow straightened.

·Protect Your Energy Field
from the Matrix
(or Mass Consciousness)

The fingers of the right hand are fully extended and touch each other. The right hand is held in front of the chest, palm facing away from the body with the fingers pointing upward. The left index finger is extended upward, and the other fingers are closed. The left index finger is held in front of the right palm.

Heal the Second Chakra So That You Can Take Balanced Action

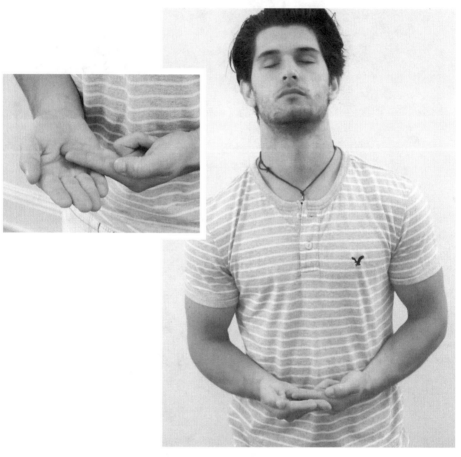

The fingers of the right hand are fully extended and touch each other. The right hand is held palm-up in front of the second chakra. The left index and middle fingers are extended and placed into the right palm (the left palm is also facing up). The left thumb is placed over the left ring and pinky fingers.

The Trinity of God

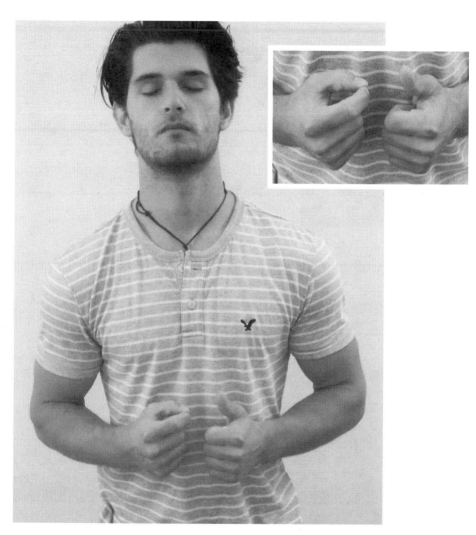

The left hand makes a fist with the thumb pointing upward. The tips of the right thumb and index finger touch, making a ring. The other fingers are closed. Both hands are held in front of the solar plexus with the palms facing toward the body and do not touch each other.
Sound: saa haa doo

Antenna Mudra
(I Am Receptive)

The left index finger extends and the other fingers of the left hand are closed. The left thumb is over the middle finger. The right index and middle fingers make a V (pointing upward), and the other fingers of the right hand are closed. The left index finger is held inside the V of the right fingers but does not touch them. Both hands are held in front of the solar plexus.

Children

Balance Mental Growth
(Where There Is No Trauma)

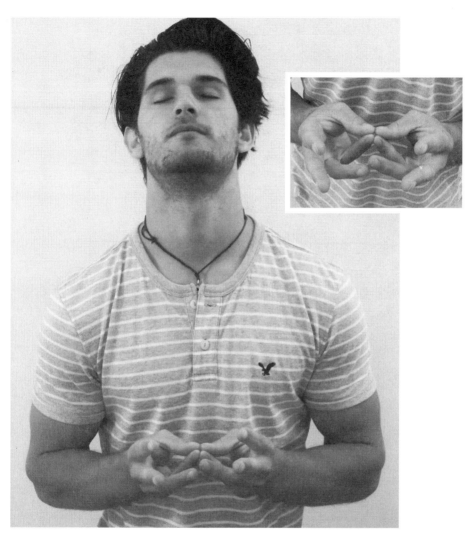

Both thumbs and pinky fingers touch each other, and the tips of these fingers on both hands touch each other as well. The other fingers are spread apart. Children play and dance with their hands held together in front of their bodies in this configuration.

Feel Safe and Secure in Your Environment

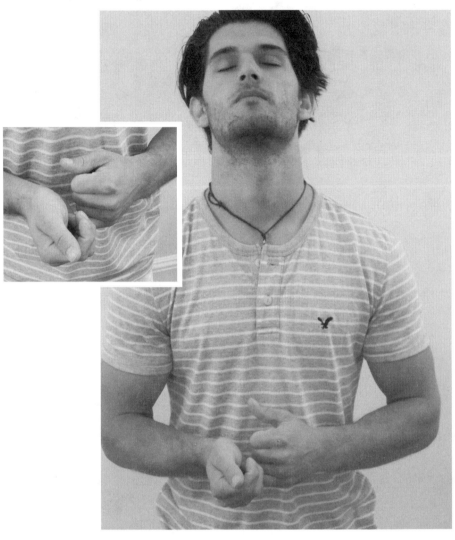

The left pinky finger hooks the right pinky finger. The thumbs and the other fingers are closed. Children play and dance with their hands held together in front of them in this configuration.

Generate Positive and Beautiful Dreams to Enhance the Imagination

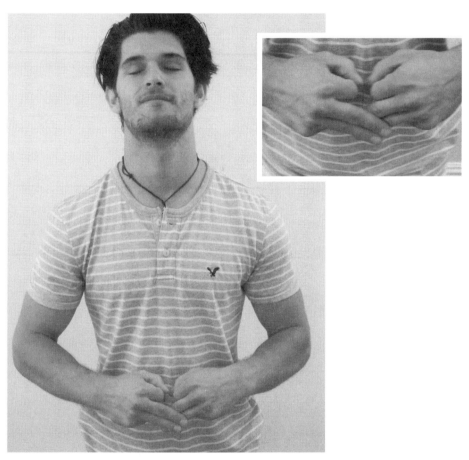

Both ring and middle fingers are extended, and thumbs and other fingers are closed. The ring and middle fingers of the right hand are held across and on top of the ring and middle fingers of the left hand, both palms down. Children play and dance with their hands held together in front of them in this configuration.

Self-Confidence and Self-Worth

Make fists with both hands, extending the thumbs upward. The left fist is placed above the right thumb. Both hands stack vertically in front of the body. Children play and dance with their hands held together in front of them in this configuration.

Inner Strength

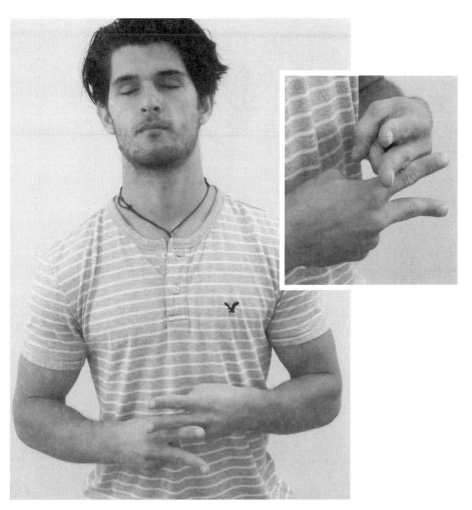

With each hand, make a V with the extended index and middle fingers pointing away from the body. The other fingers close against the palms. The left V is stacked across and above the right V, and both hands are held in front of the body. Children play and dance with their hands held together in front of them in this configuration.

Inner Self-Reliance
(Believe in Yourself)

The left index and middle fingers are extended while the remaining fingers and thumb are closed. The right hand grasps and holds the extended fingers, which are inserted into the right hand from below. The right thumb touches the tips of the right index and middle fingers. Children play and dance with their hands held together in front of them in this configuration.

Get Along with Your Peers

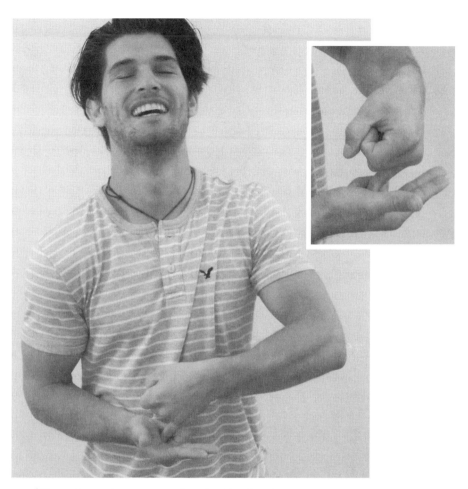

The right index and middle finders are extended as well as the thumb. The ring and pinky fingers are closed. The left index finger is extended and points downward and touches the right palm vertically. The remaining finger and thumb on the left hand are closed. Both hands are held in front of the body. Children play and dance with their hands held together in front of them in this configuration.

Create Healthy Eating Habits

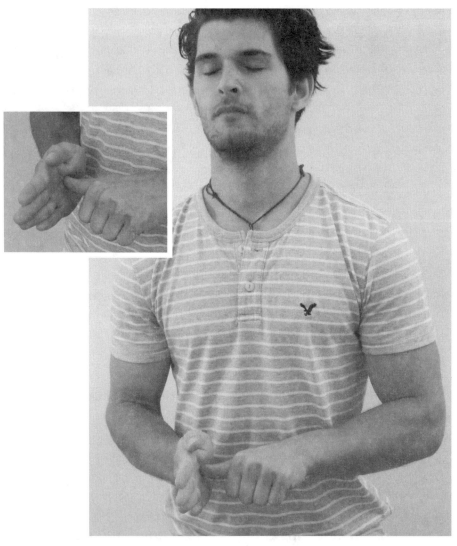

The fingers of the right hand are extended, touching each other and pointing forward. The fingers of the left hand make a fist with the left thumb extended. The left thumb touches the right palm. Children play and dance with their hands held together in front of them in this configuration.

Protection from Harmful Effects
(Television, Internet)

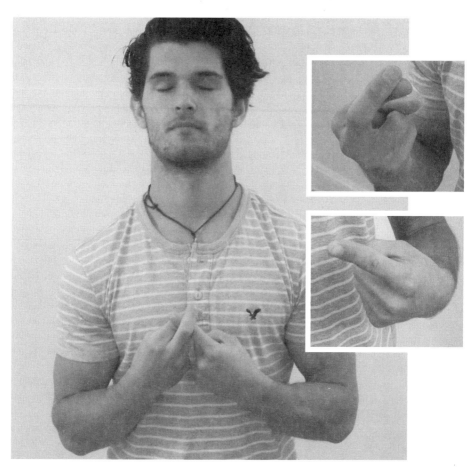

The thumb and fingers of the left hand are closed except the index finger, which is extended. Only the right middle and index fingers are extended, and the right middle finger crosses over the index finger. The left index finger is inserted between the right middle and index fingers with the palms of both hands facing the body. Children play and dance with their hands held together in front of them in this configuration.

Resolve Jealousy among Siblings

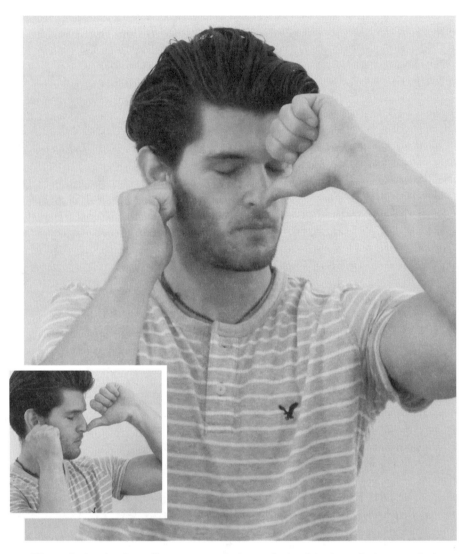

The right index finger and thumb hold the right earlobe. The extended left thumb touches the bridge of the nose, and the other fingers of the left hand are closed. Children play and dance with their hands held in this configuration.

Develop Brain Power
and Intellect

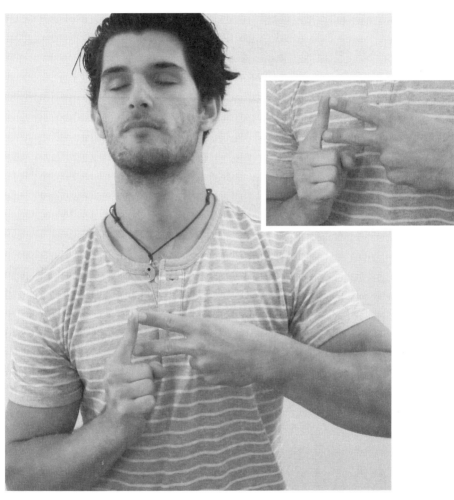

The right index finger is extended and held vertically. The left index and middle fingers make a V (palm facing the body) and touch the side of the extended right index finger. Children play and dance with their hands held together in front of them in this configuration.

Calm Overaggressiveness

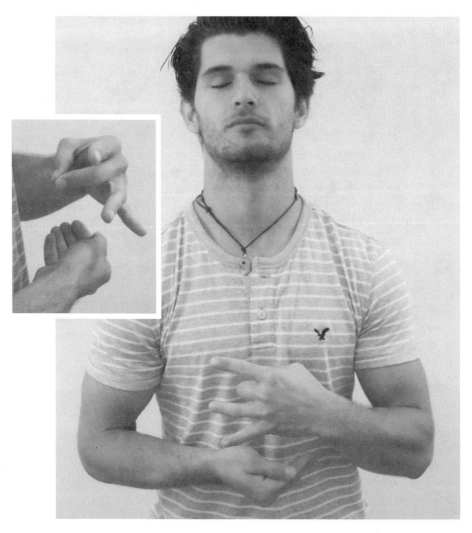

Cup the right hand and hold it palm-up in front of the body. The tip of the left thumb touches the tip of the left middle finger, making a ring. The other left fingers extend. This ring is held parallel over the right palm. The hands do not touch. Children play and dance with their hands in front of them in this configuration.

Calm Hyperactivity

The left hand makes a fist. The right index finger extends downward and touches the top of the left fist. Children play and dance with their hands held together in front of them in this configuration.

Motivation

The right hand is cupped and held in front of the body, palm up. The tip of the left thumb touches the tips of the left index, middle, and ring fingers. The left pinky finger extends. The left hand is held over the cupped right hand. All fingertips point in the same direction (away from the body). Their hands do not touch. Children play and dance with their hands in front of them in this configuration.

Healthy Digestion and Elimination

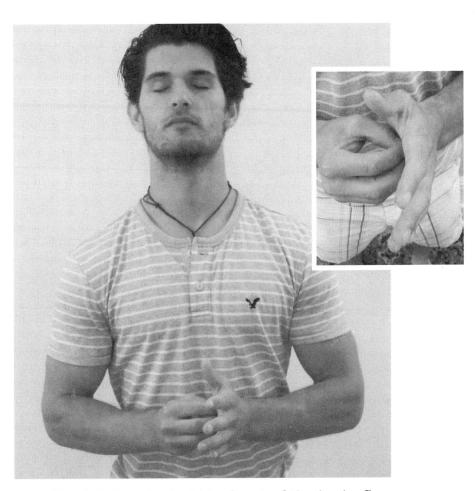

The left hand is held in front of the body, fingers extended and not touching. The right fingers are bent, barely touching each other, and the tips of the right fingers nestle into the palm of the left hand. The palms face toward each other. Children play and dance with their hands held together in front of them in this configuration.

DNA Activation

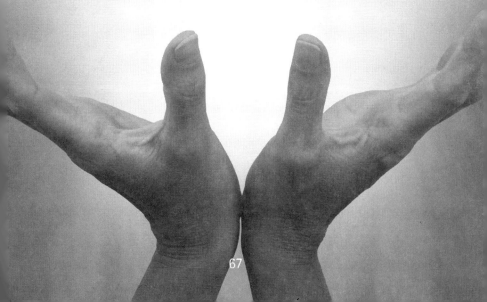

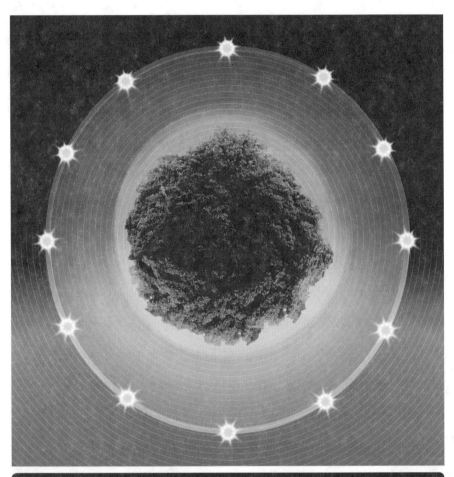

Layer 1: Tree of Life

Layer 1: Tree of Life

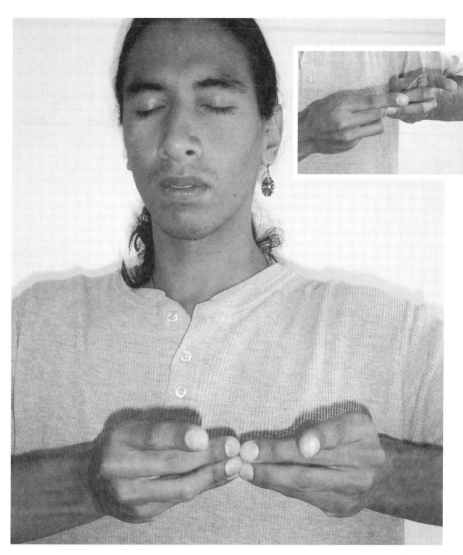

The thumb touches the tips of the middle, ring, and pinky fingers on both hands, which come together to touch at these fingertips. The index fingers do not touch anything and are extended, pointing away from the body. Both hands are held horizontally in front of the heart.

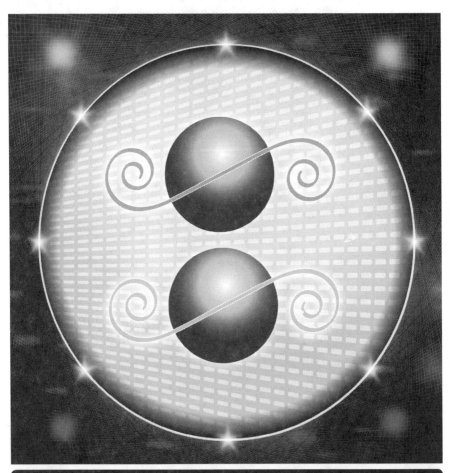

Layer 2: Blueprint of Life

Layer 2: Blueprint of Life

Both middle and pinky fingers are closed, touching the palms. Both thumbs touch the index and ring fingers. Both hands are held over the heart (palms toward the body) with the tips of the index and ring fingers touching.

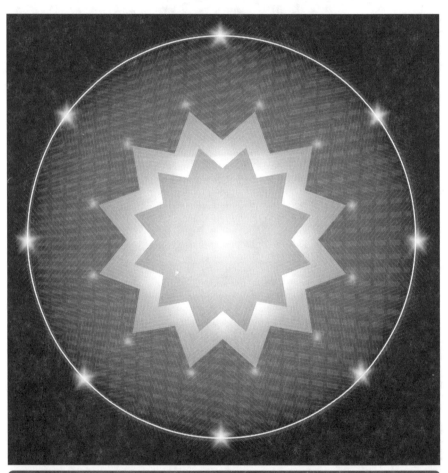

Layer 3: Present Consciousness Awakening

Layer 3: Present Consciousness Awakening

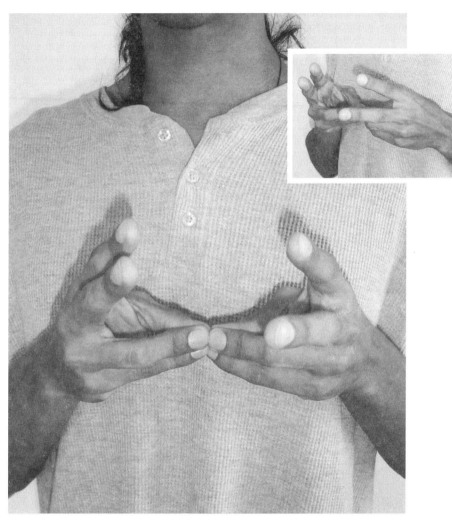

Both thumbs touch the ring and pinky fingers. The index and middle fingers do not touch and are extended. Both hands come together at the fingertips in front of the heart chakra, and the middle and index fingers point away from the body.

Layer 4: Belief

Layer 4: Belief

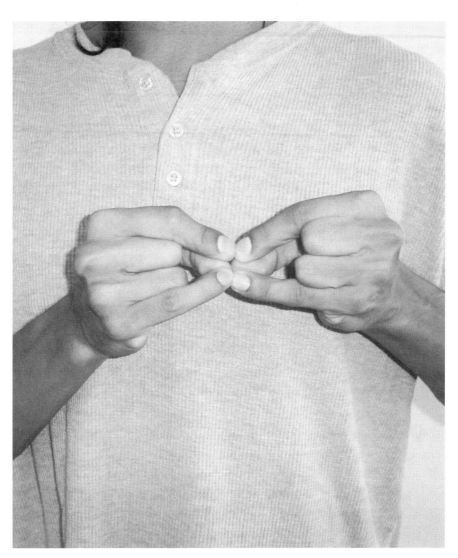

Both middle and ring fingers are bent down and touch the palms. The thumbs of both hands touch the index and pinky fingers. The extended fingertips touch and both hands are placed between the heart and the stomach area.

Layer 5: Awakening Self

Layer 5: Awakening Self

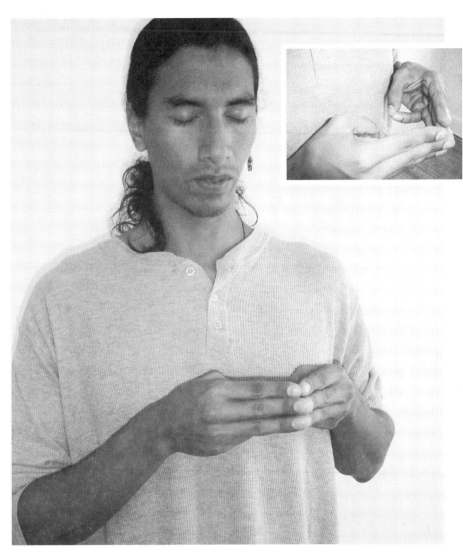

Both thumbs touch the pinky fingers. The index, middle, and ring fingers are extended and kept close together. The tips of the extended fingers come together. Both hands are in front of the heart with the extended fingers pointing away from the body.

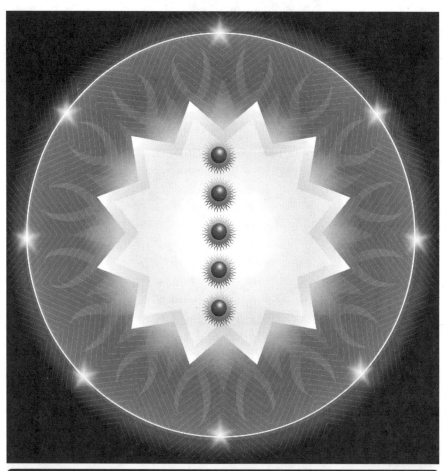

Layer 6: I Am That I Am

Layer 6: I Am That I Am

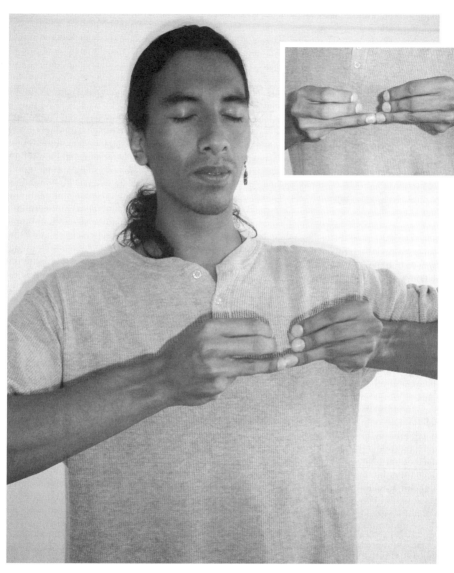

Both thumbs touch the index and middle fingers. The pinky fingers are closed and touch the palms. The tips of the ring fingers touch. Hands are held over the heart area with the palms facing the body.

Layer 7: Balance

Layer 7: Balance

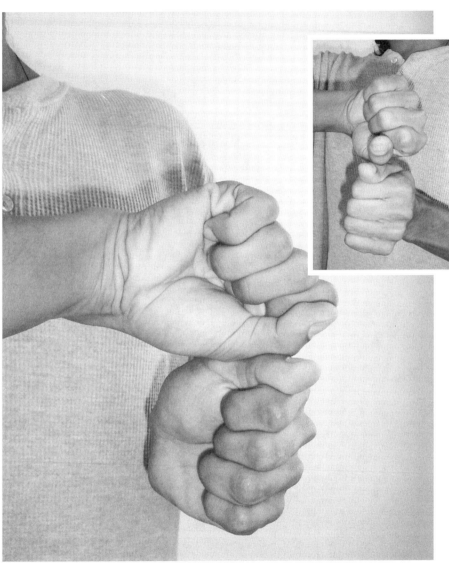

*The hands form two fists, thumbs flat, not curled.
The right hand is stacked atop the left, and both
palms face right. Both fists are held vertically in
front of the heart.*

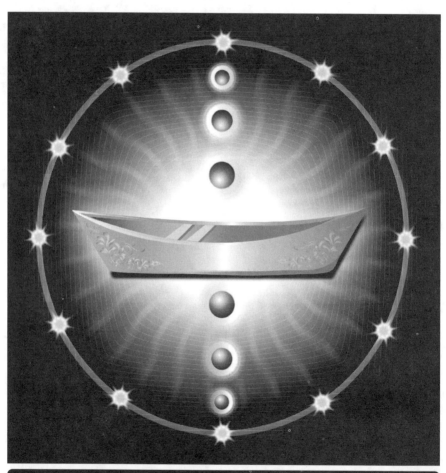

Layer 8: Truth

Layer 8: Truth

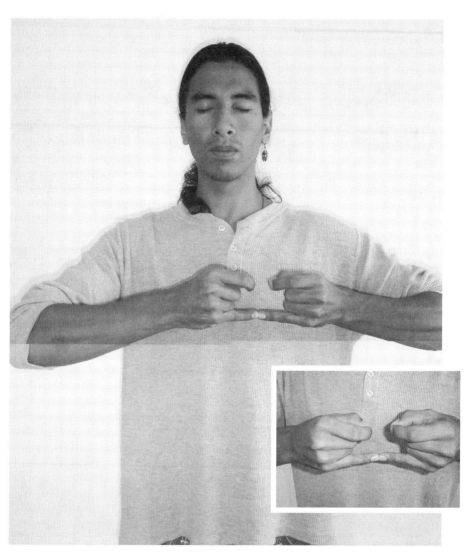

Both thumbs touch the index fingers. The middle and ring fingers are bent down into the palms, and the tips of both pinky fingers touch each other. The hands are held horizontally in front of the heart area with the palms toward the body.

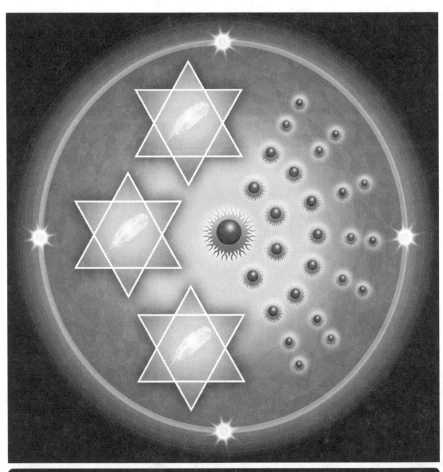

Layer 9: Opening the Grand Eye

Layer 9: Opening the Grand Eye

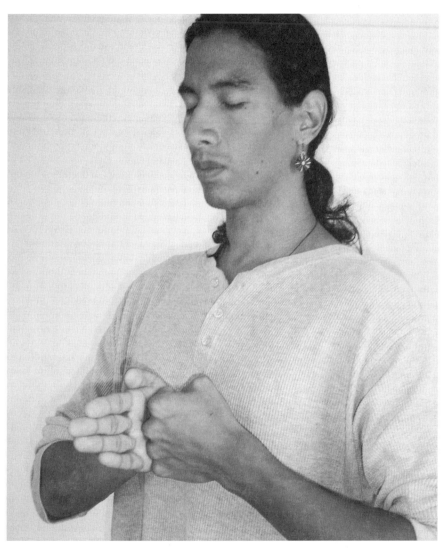

The left hand forms a fist with no gaps between the fingers. The right hand is extended, fingers closed, from the body. The knuckles of the left hand are placed in the palm of the right hand. The hands are held in front of the heart area.

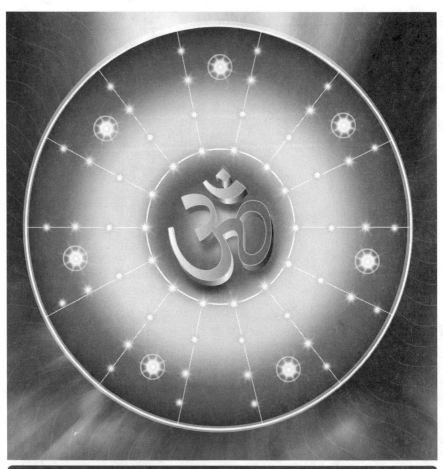

Layer 10: Remembrance

Layer 10: Remembrance

The left hand forms a fist with the thumb up. The fingers of the right hand are splayed and the thumbs touch. The hands are held in front of the heart with the thumbs pointing upward.

Layer 11: Realization

Layer 11: Realization

Both hands form fists and hook at the thumbs, right hand on top (palm away from body) and left hand on bottom (palm toward body). The hands are held vertically in front of the heart.

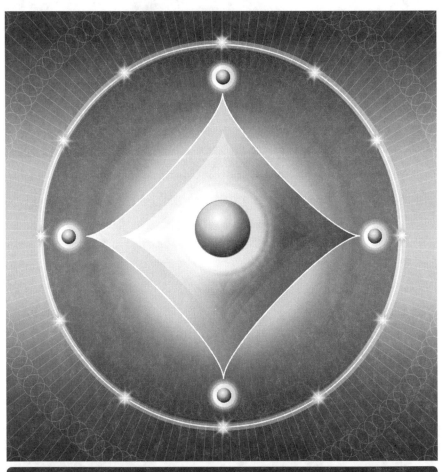

Layer 12: God

Layer 12: God

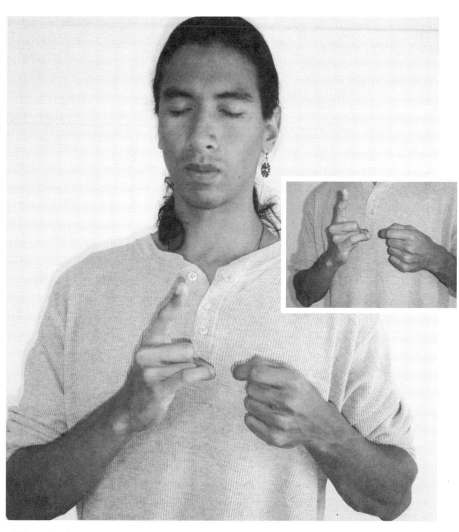

The right thumb and pinky finger touch. The right index finger is raised, and the middle and ring fingers are closed. The left thumb touches the left index finger, and the other fingers are closed, making a circle that should face upward. Hold both hands — not touching each other — in front of the heart.

Healing Earth

Release Blocks in Earth's Energy Meridians

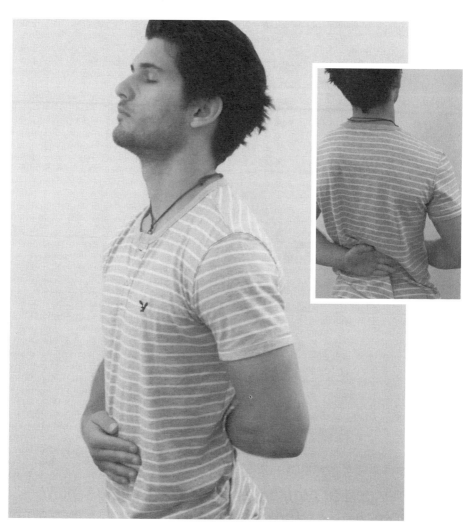

Fingers are extended and closed on both hands. The right palm is held over the solar plexus. The back of the left hand is held against the back, directly behind the right hand. Focus attention on the third eye.
Sound: sssaaammm vvyyoo

Send Love to Mother Earth

*The fingers of both hands are extended and separated
from each other. The right hand is held on the left-front
side of the body so that the fingertips touch the left
shoulder. The left hand is held out in front of the body
with the elbow bent and arm touching the left side of
the body. Focus attention on the solar plexus.
Sound: aaarrrr ddhh*

Support All Creation on Earth
(Plants, Animals)

Both hands form fists (thumbs on top). The right arm extends straight in front of the body. The left fist touches the right collarbone. Focus attention on the heart.
Sound: kkaallvveeee

Cleanse the Ground So That We Can Feel Love from Mother Earth

The right hand is held in front of the right side of the body with the elbow bent. All fingers and thumb are open and separated, and the palm faces away from the body. The tips of the left thumb and index finger touch, making a circle. The other fingers of the left hand are spread apart and extended. The left hand is held in front of the right palm. Focus attention on the third eye.
Sound: mmuurrddhhaa

Protect Mother Earth from Humanity's Activities
(Pollution, Excavation, and so forth)

The fingers of the right hand are splayed. The right hand is held so that the palm faces away from the body, elbow bent. The tips of the left index finder and thumb touch to make a ring. The other fingers of the left hand extend and are separated. The ring made by the left hand is held in front of the right palm. Both hands do not touch and are held in front of the chest. Focus attention between the heart and solar plexus.
Sound: aarruumm

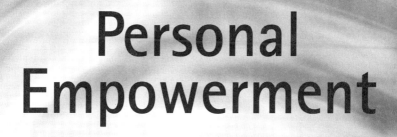

Personal
Empowerment

Bring Back Lost Parts
of Your Consciousness

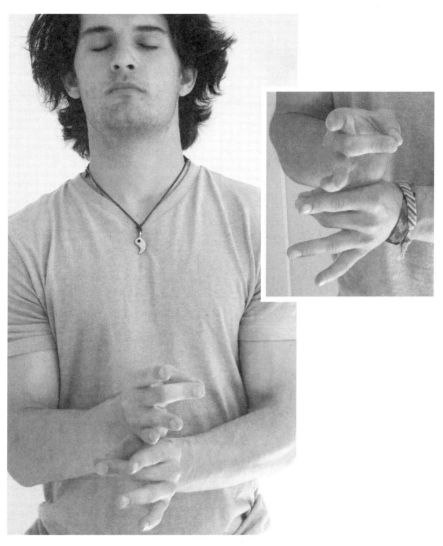

*Both thumbs touch the middle fingers. The other fingers
are separated and point forward. The right hand rests atop
the left hand (right pinky over left thumb and index finger).
Both hands are held in front of the solar plexus.*

I Am Strong and Can Overcome All Obstacles in My Life

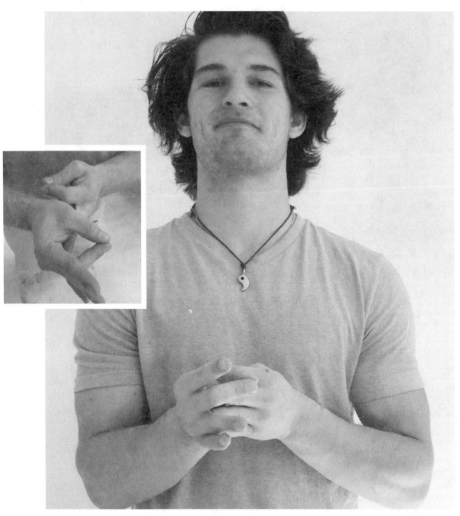

The right middle finger touches the right thumb, and the other fingers are extended. The left index finger touches the left thumb. The extended fingers of the left hand rest in the palm of the right hand. Both hands are held in front of the solar plexus.

I Am Responsible

The fingers of the left hand are extended, closed, and pointing away from the body. The middle right finger and thumb touch each other and are held touching the left palm. The other fingers are extended and pointing forward.

I Generate Wisdom in My Life

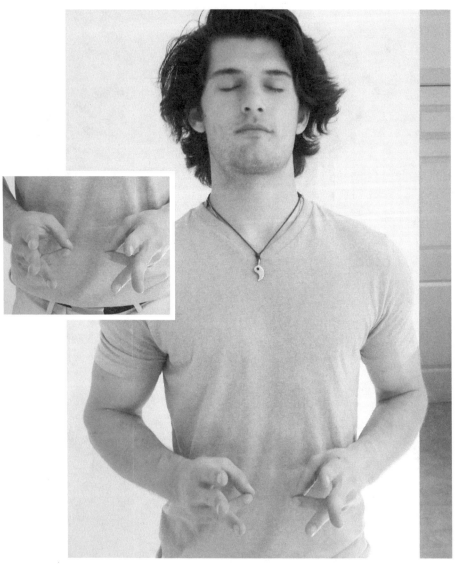

Pinky fingers and thumbs touch on both hands (all other fingers are extended) and held separately in front of the solar plexus with the fingers pointing forward.

Right and Left Brain Integration

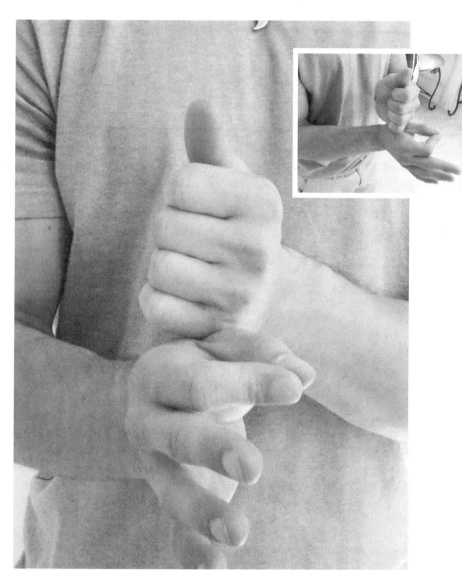

The right thumb and index fingers touch with the other fingers extended and separated. The left hand forms a fist and rests atop the right hand. Both hands are held in front of the body.

I Am the Power and the Force

The right hand makes a fist with the thumb resting on top. The left hand makes a fist with the thumb extended upward. The left hand rests on the right hand. Both are held in front of the solar plexus.

Responsible
Creation

Open the Infinite Heart within Me

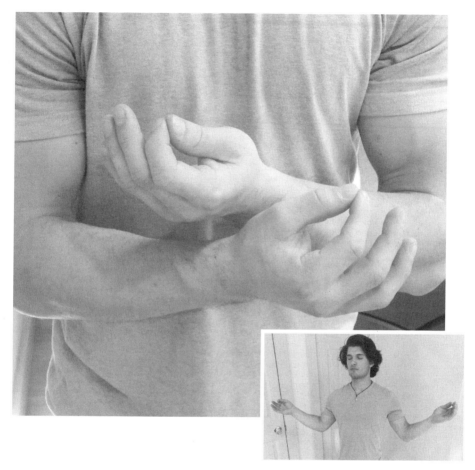

I. The index fingers and thumbs of both hands touch. The wrists cross — palms up — in front of the solar plexus with the left hand above the right hand.

II. Open both arms in a fluid motion, keeping the elbows bent.

Balance of Heaven and Earth

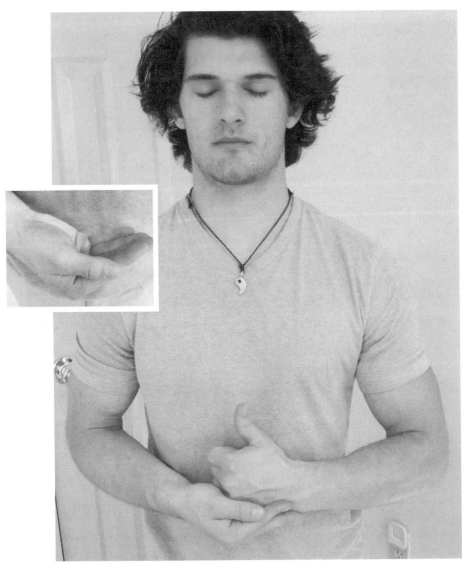

The right hand is cupped. The left hand forms a fist with the thumb extended upward and sits in the cupped right hand. Both hands are held in front of the solar plexus.

Ground Your Consciousness to Be Able to Manifest Ideas

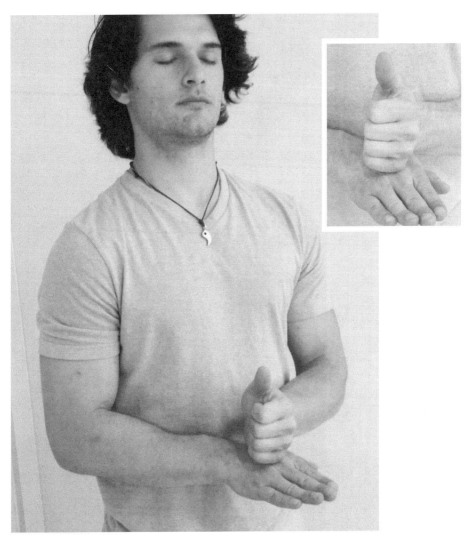

The fingers of the right hand are closed and extend away from the body with the palm facing downward. The left hand forms a fist with the thumb extended upward. The left hand rests on the back of the right. Both are held in front of the solar plexus.

I Am Open and Flexible

Both middle fingers wrap around the index fingers with the thumbs extended upward and the ring and pinky fingers turned toward the palm. The middle and index fingers of the left hand rest on top of the right with the palms facing the body.

Disentangle from Drama

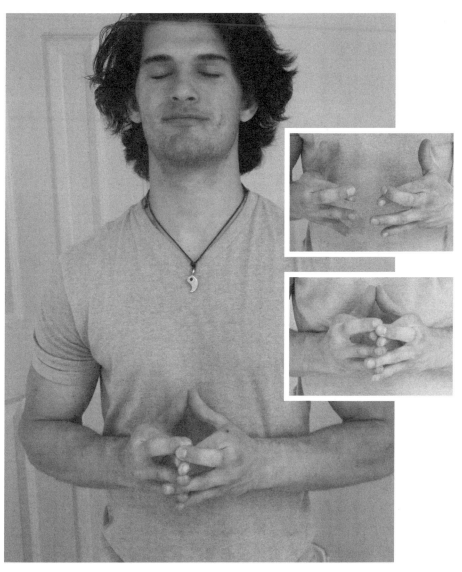

Both middle fingers wrap around the index fingers. The other fingers are splayed, thumbs extending upward. Both hands come together in front of the solar plexus, thumbs touching and fingertips interlaced.

Ability to Ask for Help

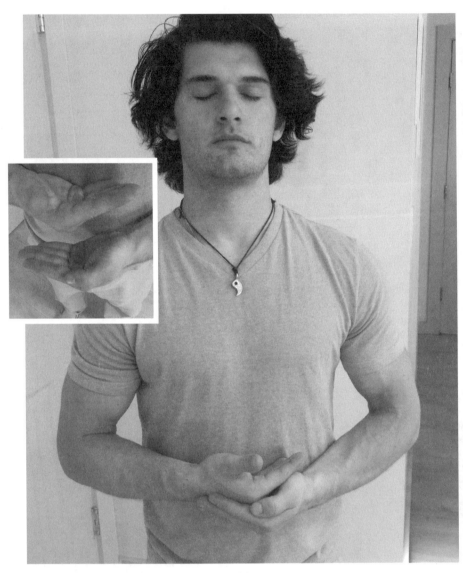

*Both hands are cupped with the right thumb
extended forward away from the body. The right
hand sits in the cupped left hand. Both hands are
held in front of the solar plexus.*

Ability to Share

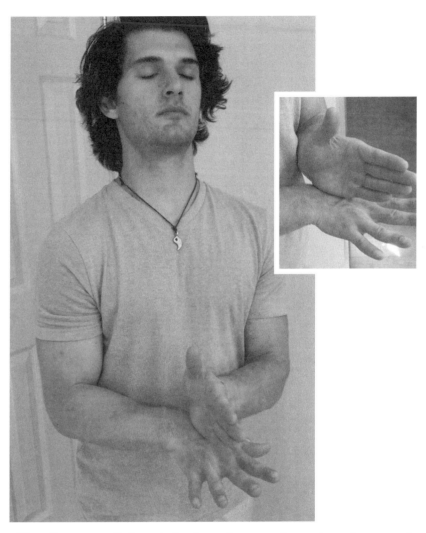

The fingers of the right hand are splayed and extend away from the body, palm down. The fingers of the left hand are extended and closed, pointing forward with the thumb extending upward. The left hand rests on the back of the right hand. Both hands are held in front of the solar plexus.

Ability to Know When to Go Forward and When to Pull Back

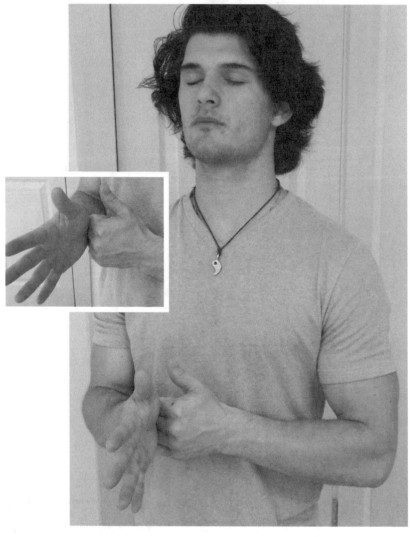

The fingers of the right hand are splayed and extend away from the body, thumb pointing upward. The left hand forms a fist, thumb pointing upward, and the knuckles touch the right wrist. Both hands are held in front of the solar plexus.

Generate the Energy of Stillness

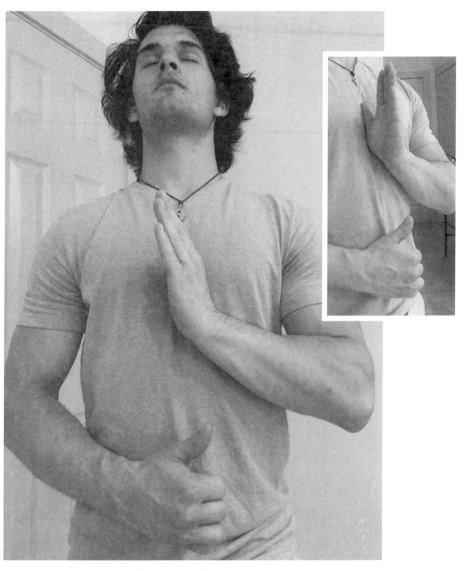

The right hand forms a fist with the thumb extending upward, held in front of the navel. The fingers of the left hand are closed and extended upward, separated from the thumb and held in front of the sternum.

I Am Complete in Myself, and I Do Not Get Lost in Another Person

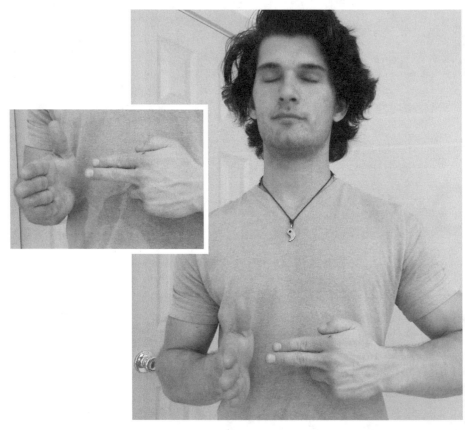

The fingers of the right hand are closed and extended away from the body with the thumb pointing upward. The thumb, index, and middle finger of the left hand are closed and extended, pointing toward (but not touching) the right palm. The pinky finger and ring fingers of the left hand are turned toward the palm. Both hands are held in front of the solar plexus.

I Bloom Like a Flower in My Own Inner Beauty

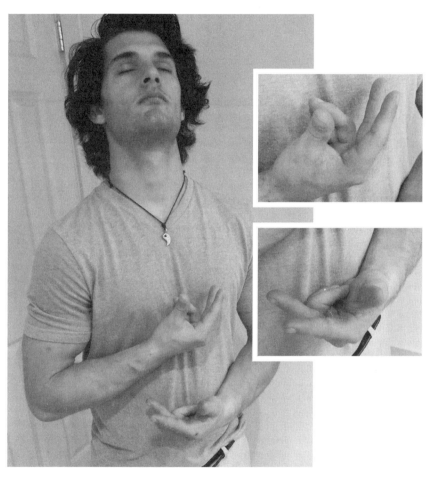

The pinky and ring fingers on the left hand touch the palm. The left hand is held in front of the navel, palm facing up, with the thumb, and remaining fingers extended separately. The right hand is held in a similar configuration with the pinky and ring fingers slightly bent, not touching the palm. The right palm faces upward and is held in front of the sternum.

Face Your Problems

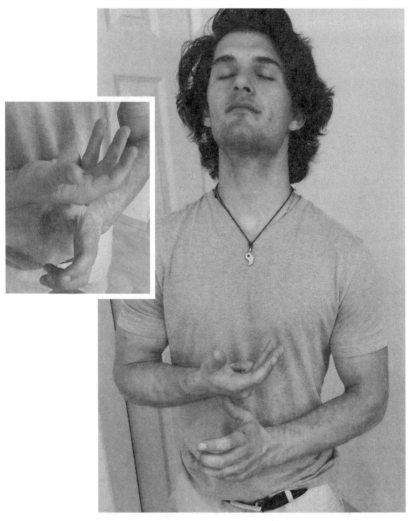

The pinky finger of the right hand touches the palm. The other fingers are splayed. The right palm faces upward in front of the solar plexus. The fingers of the left hand are slightly curled and lightly touching, with the left thumb extended upward. The right hand rests on top of the left thumb.

Ascension

I Am Complete: the God/ Goddess (Masculine/Feminine) within Me Are Integrated

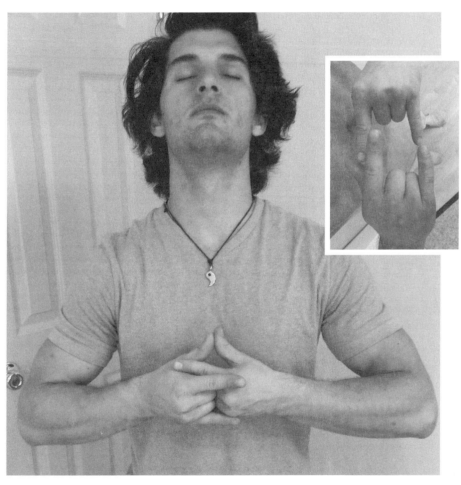

Both middle and ring fingers touch the palms, and the index and pinky fingers extend outward. Hands are brought together (knuckles touch and splayed fingers overlap) in front of the solar plexus, thumbs touching and pointing upward.

Soul Integration: I Am the Soul

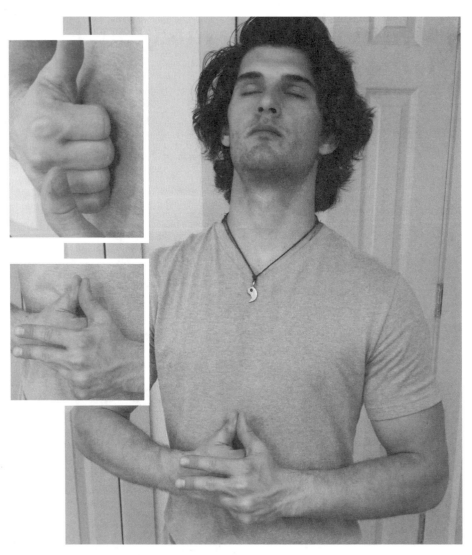

The right hand forms a fist, thumb up, held in front of the solar plexus. The ring and pinky fingers of the left hand touch the left palm, and the index and middle fingers extend separately to touch the back of the right hand. Both thumbs touch and point upward.

I Am the Monad

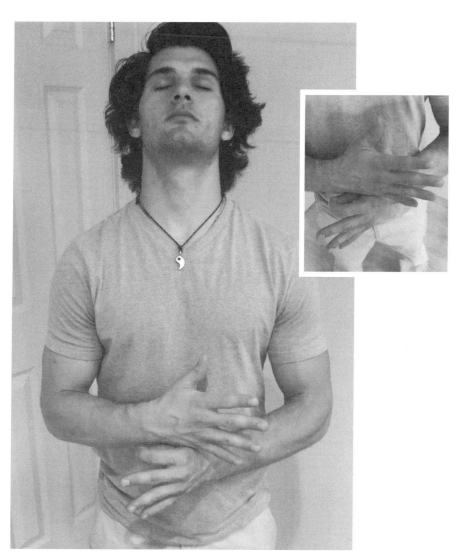

The fingers of the right hand are splayed with the thumb pointing upward. The tips of the thumb and index finger of the left hand touch, and the other fingers are splayed. The right hand crosses over the left at the wrist. Both hands are held in front of the solar plexus.

I Am the Presence

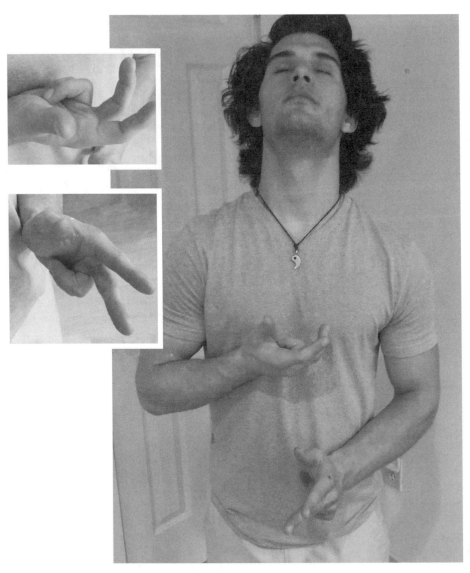

Both ring and pinky fingers touch the palms, and the other fingers are splayed. The left hand is held in front of the navel, fingers pointing forward, and the right hand is held palm-up in front of the sternum.

I Am Mahatma, Great Soul

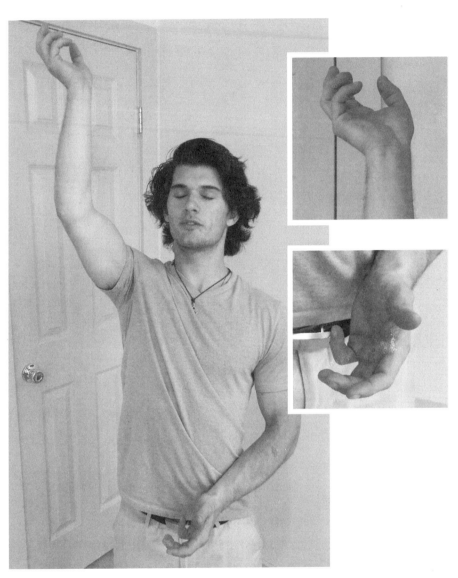

The fingers of both hands are separated and loosely curled. The right arm is extended above the head (elbow relaxed and palm up), and the left hand is held close to the body in front of the second chakra.

Climb the 352-Rung Ladder to the God Level

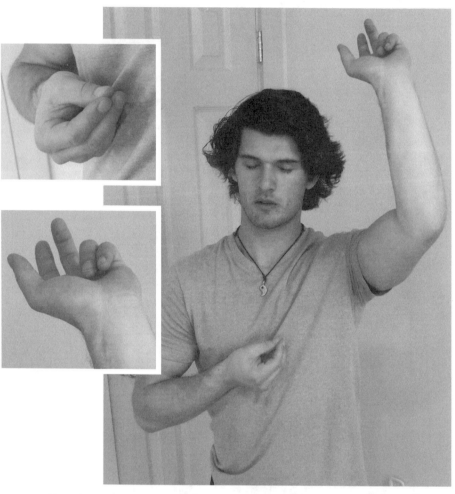

The four fingers of the right hand touch the thumb. The ring and pinky fingers of the left hand touch the palm, and the other fingers and the thumb extend separately. The right hand is held in front of the heart, and the left hand is held above the head, palm up, elbow bent, facing forward.

Access the Creative Power of the Goddess

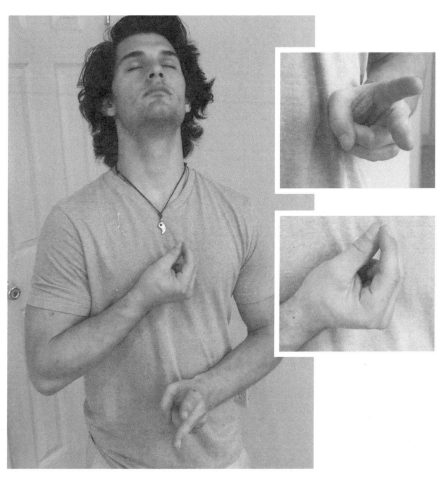

The left thumb is held over the left ring and pinky fingers. The left index and middle fingers are splayed, forming a V and pointing away from the body, held in front of the solar plexus. The right pinky and ring fingers touch the palm, and the index and middle fingers touch the thumb. The right hand is held palm-up in front of the sternum.

I Am Truly Balanced

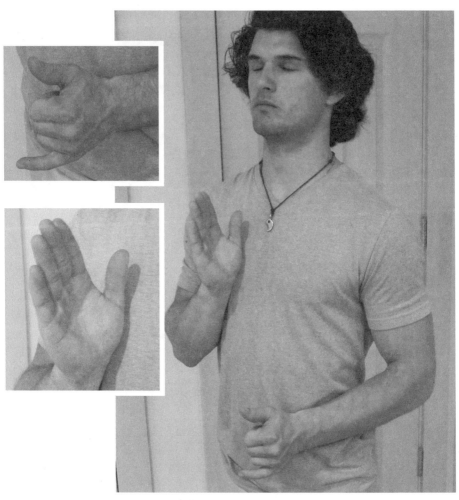

The fingers of the right hand are extended, closed, separated from the thumb, and held in front of the sternum with the fingertips pointed upward. The index, middle, and ring fingers of the left hand touch the palm. The pinky finger and thumb are extended. The upper left arm rests against the body, and the elbow is bent, pointing the extended left fingers forward.

I Connect with the Most Important Force in My Body, "La Banahah"

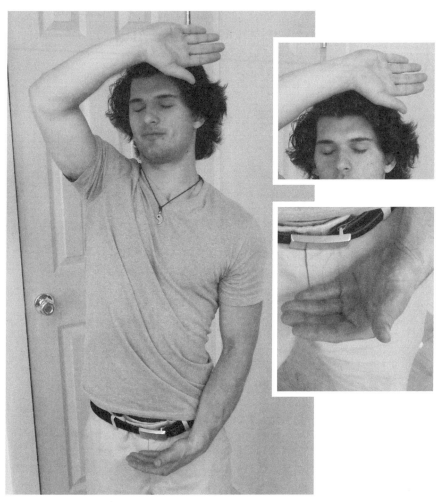

The fingers of the right hand are closed and extended, held palm-out above the forehead. The fingers of the left hand are slightly cupped and held palm-up at the second chakra.

I Connect with the Sun within Me

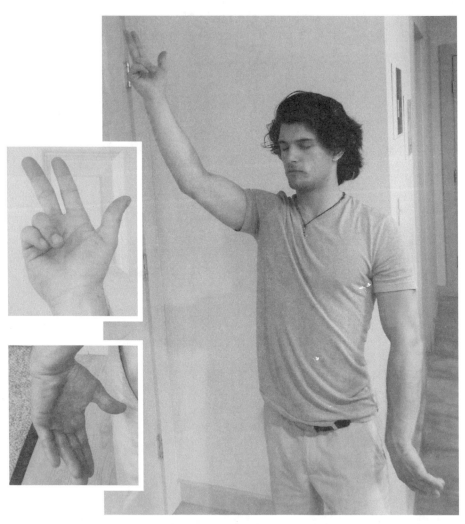

The fingers of the left hand are closed and extended, held below the waist with the palm facing back. The pinky and ring fingers of the right hand are bent inward, and the index and middle fingers and thumb are splayed. The right hand is held forward and above the head.

I Integrate with All the Energies I Have Awakened within Me

The fingers and thumb of the right hand are closed and extended, pointing away from the body at chest height. The left index finger points upward to (and touches) the bottom of the right wrist. The other fingers are closed with the thumb touching the middle finger.

I Call Forth and Connect with All the Supporting Energies Available to Me

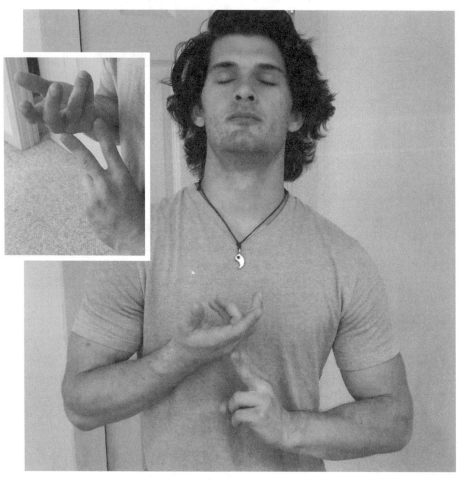

The right ring finger wraps around the right pinky finger. The other fingers and thumb are open and slightly curled with the palm facing up. The left index and middle fingers make a V and touch the back of the right hand. The left thumb wraps over the left ring finger.

About Rae Chandran

Rae Chandran was born in India and has lived in the United States and Japan. He performs individual channeling sessions for his clients, and he has published articles in the *Sedona Journal of Emergence!* Rae teaches workshops throughout the Far East on the Ancient Egyptian mysteries, DNA activation, and channeling. He creates soul symbols for his clients, and he leads tours of ancient holy places worldwide.

Rae founded the Omran Institute, which promotes DNA awareness and certifies practitioners of Omran 12-Strand DNA Activation. He also performs individual Omran 12-Strand DNA sessions for clients. Rae lives with his wife and children outside of Tokyo, Japan. Visit his website at www .RaeChandran.com.

About Robert Mason Pollock

Robert Mason Pollock was born in Washington, DC, and has lived in London (England), Canada, and the Berkshire mountains of Massachusetts. He is an energy healer at a holistic health resort in the Berkshires, and he has an energy healing practice with locations in New York City and the Berkshires.

Robert wrote *Navigating by Heart.* He teaches workshops in spirituality and DNA activation. He also performs individual Omran 12-Strand DNA sessions for clients. Robert currently lives in the Berkshires, and his website is www.BerkshireEnergyHealing.com.

RAE CHANDRAN

A practical guide to reconnecting with your divine blueprint

CHANNELED BY **Rae Chandran**
WITH **Robert Mason Pollock**

$19.95 • Softcover • 384 PP. • ISBN: 978-1-62233-013-3

32 color pages of mudras and images to activate your 12 levels of DNA

DNA of the Spirit, Volume 1

The etheric strands of your DNA are the information library of your soul. They contain the complete history of you, lifetime after lifetime; a record of the attitudes, karma, and emotional predispositions you brought into this lifetime; and a blueprint, or lesson plan, for your self-improvement. Your DNA is also a record of your existence from the moment of your creation as a starbeing to your present incarnation. This information is written in every cell of your body.

CHAPTERS INCLUDE:

- Mudras for Activating the Twelve Layers of DNA
- The Awakening of Crystalline Consciousness
- Auspicious Times for Awakening Consciousness
- Angelic Support for DNA Activation
- The History of Human DNA
- Your Internal Compass: Nature's Body Intelligence

Phone: 928-526-1345 or 1-800-450-0985 • Fax: 928-714-1132

RAE CHANDRAN

$16.95 • Softcover • 192 PP. • 978-1-62233-027-0

DNA of the Spirit, Volume 2

This companion book to *DNA of the Spirit, Vol. 1* originated with the intention and desire to bring forth understanding to support humanity. Go through this volume while holding a sacredness inside of you, asking that the material be imprinted in your sacredness so that it may become an experience that you will be able to live.

Some of the material in this book is coded, and sincere students will find they can open these codes. Understanding can be received through your own filter and in your own way. This way, you will find the Divine within.

CHAPTERS INCLUDE:

- Auric Imprinting Technique for Healing
- The Number of God
- Reveal Your Life Contracts
- Re-create Your Life with Your Akashic Records
- Humans Are Creators in Training
- Use Shape-Shifting for Regeneration
- How to Activate the Codes Within You
- From Darkness unto Light: the Aquarian Age
- Discover Your Energy Connections to Beings of Light
- Understand the Sacred Geometry of the Human Body
- Determine What Drives Your Soul

RAE CHANDRAN

PARTNER WITH ANGELS

And Benefit Every Area of Your Life

channeled by Rae Chandran
with Robert Mason Pollock

$16.95 • Softcover • 208 pp. • 978-1-62233-034-8

CHAPTERS INCLUDE:

- The Benefits of Working with Angels
- Prepare for a New Consciousness
- Design Your Unique Path
- Access Support from Celestial Bodies
- Invoke Vibrational Support and Activation
- Practice Universal Communication
- Develop Environmental Connections
- You Are the New Masters

Partner with Angels and Benefit Every Area of Your Life

Angels are the Creator's workforce, and in this book, individual angels describe their responsibilities and explain how they can help you with all aspects of your life — practical and spiritual. All you need to do is ask.

Many of these angels have never spoken to human beings before or revealed their names or what they do. Here are some examples of what you will find inside:

- **La Banaha**, the essence of the Moon, explains feminine empowerment and organ rejuvenation.
- **Angel Anauel** describes fair commerce.
- **Angel Tahariel** helps you purify and shift your vibration.
- **Angel Mansu** gives advice about how to eliminate the trauma from birthing procedures.
- **Angel Agon** inspires writers and filmmakers and relates how you can call on him for inspiration.
- **Angel Tadzekiel** helps you access your own wisdom and put it into perspective.
- **Archangel Maroni** downloads your individual pathway to ascension.

The purpose of this material is to bring the awareness of angels in a much more practical, easy-to-understand way. Call on the angels to show you all the potential you have in your life to create a new reality.

Phone: 928-526-1345 or 1-800-450-0985 • Fax: 928-714-1132

⚜ *Light Technology* PUBLISHING

TOM T. MOORE

THE GENTLE WAY
A SELF-HELP GUIDE FOR THOSE WHO BELIEVE IN ANGELS

This book will put you back in touch with your guardian angel or strengthen and expand the connection that you already have. How can I promise these benefits? Because I have been using these concepts for years and I can report these successes from direct knowledge and experience.

$14.⁹⁵ • 160 PP., SOFTCOVER • ISBN 978-1-891824-60-9

THE GENTLE WAY II
BENEVOLENT OUTCOMES: THE STORY CONTINUES

You'll be amazed at how easy it is to be in touch with guardian angels and how much assistance you can receive simply by asking. This inspirational self-help book, written for all faiths and beliefs, will explain how there is a more benevolent world that we can access and how we can achieve this.

$16.⁹⁵ • 320 PP., SOFTCOVER • ISBN 978-1-891824-80-7

THE GENTLE WAY III
MASTER YOUR LIFE

I continue to receive truly unique stories from people all over the world requesting most benevolent outcomes and asking for benevolent prayers for their families, friends, other people, and other beings. It just proves that there are no limits to this modality, which is becoming a gentle movement as people discover how much better their lives are with these simple yet powerful requests.

$16.⁹⁵ • 352 PP., SOFTCOVER • ISBN 978-1-62233-005-8

FIRST CONTACT
CONVERSATIONS WITH AN ET

This book contains vital information about our past, present, and future contact with ETs. Tom relays this information through conversations with "his brother from another planet," Antura.

$15.⁹⁵ • 224 PP., SOFTCOVER • ISBN 978-1-62233-004-1

ATLANTIS & LEMURIA
THE LOST CONTINENTS REVEALED!

Sixty thousand years ago, Earth had two more continents than it does today, each larger than what we now know as Australia. Why are they no longer there?

$16.⁹⁵ • 256 PP., SOFTCOVER • ISBN 978-1-62233-037-9

by Cheryl Gaer Barlow

✤ *Light Technology* PUBLISHING

DRUNVALO MELCHIZEDEK

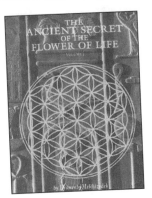

THE ANCIENT SECRET OF THE FLOWER OF LIFE
VOLUME 1

Once, all life in the universe knew the Flower of Life as the creation pattern, the geometrical design leading us into and out of physical existence. Then from a very high state of consciousness, we fell into darkness, and the secret was hidden for thousands of years, encoded in the cells of all life.

$25.⁰⁰ • 240 PP. SOFTCOVER • ISBN 978-1-891824-17-3

THE ANCIENT SECRET OF THE FLOWER OF LIFE
VOLUME 2

Finally, for the first time in print, Drunvalo shares the instructions for the Mer-Ka-Ba meditation, step-by-step techniques for the re-creation of the energy field of the evolved human, which is the key to ascension and the next dimensional world. If done from love, this ancient process of breathing prana opens up for us a world of tantalizing possibility in this dimension, from protective powers to the healing of oneself, of others, and even of the planet.

$25.⁰⁰ • 272 PP. SOFTCOVER • ISBN 978-1-891824-21-0

LIVING IN THE HEART
Includes Heart Meditation CD

"Long ago we humans used a form of communication and sensing that did not involve the brain in any way; rather, it came from a sacred place within our hearts. What good would it do to find this place again in a world where the greatest religion is science and the logic of the mind? Don't I know this world where emotions and feelings are second-class citizens? Yes, I do. But my teachers have asked me to remind you who you really are. You are more than a human being, much more. For within your heart is a place, a sacred place, where the world can literally be remade through conscious cocreation. If you give me permission, I will show you what has been shown to me." — Drunvalo Melchizedek

$25.⁰⁰ • 144 PP. SOFTCOVER • ISBN 978-1-891824-43-2

Shifting Frequencies
Sounds for Vibratory Activation
by Jonathan Goldman

with CD

For the first time, Healing Sounds pioneer Jonathan Goldman tells us about shifting frequencies — how to use sound and other modalities to change vibrational patterns for both personal and planetary healing and transformation. Through his consciousness connection to Shamael, angel of sound, Jonathan shares his extraordinary scientific and spiritual knowledge and insights, providing information, instructions, and techniques on using sound, light, color, visualization, and sacred geometry to experience shifting frequencies. The material in this book is both timely and vital for health and spiritual evolution.

$17⁹⁵
Plus Shipping

ISBN 978-1-891824-70-8
Softcover • 226 PP.
6 X 9 Perfect Bound

CHAPTERS INCLUDE:

- Sound Currents: Frequency and Intent
- Vibratory Resonance
- Vocalization, Visualization, and a Tonal Language
- The Harmonics of Sound
- Vocal Harmonics and Listening
- Energy Fields
- Creating Sacred Space

Hearing the Angels Sing:
A True Story of Angelic Assistance
by Peter Sterling

MUSIC CD INCLUDED

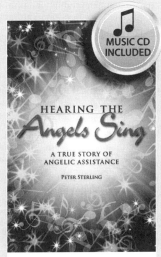

Hearing the Angel's Sing chronicles my extraordinary journeys into the higher dimensions of light where I met the angels who ultimately brought me to the realization that my mission was to be a channel for God's heavenly music. The book includes never-before-shared details of my journey of awakening. From the snowcapped peaks of the Rocky Mountains to the tropical jungles of the Mayan temple lands, the red rock towers of Sedona, and ultimately to the Incan highlands of Peru, this is a captivating story that will take you on an amazing journey of discovery!

— Peter Sterling

$16⁹⁵
Plus Shipping

ISBN 13: 978-1-891824-96-8
Softcover • 256 PP.
6 X 9 Perfect Bound

CHAPTERS INCLUDE:

- Descension and Birth
- Down the Rabbit Hole
- Windows to Heaven
- Rocky Mountain High
- Angels and Devils
- Harmonic Converging
- Red Rocks Calling
- To Hear the Angels Sing
- Fires of Purification

☽ *Light Technology* PUBLISHING *Presents*

BOOKS BY DAVID K. MILLER

Arcturians: How to Heal, Ascend, and Help Planet Earth

Go on a mind-expanding journey to explore new spiritual tools for dealing with our planetary crisis. Included in this book are new and updated interpretations of the Kaballistic Tree of Life, which has now been expanded to embrace fifth-dimensional planetary healing methods. Learn new and expanded Arcturian spiritual technologies.

$16.95 • 352 PP. • Softcover • 978-1-62233-002-7

Kaballah and the Ascension

"Throughout Western history, channeling has come to us in various forms, including mediumship, shamanism, fortunetelling, visionaries, and oracles. There is also a long history of channeling in Kaballah, the major branch of Jewish mysticism. I am intrigued by this, especially because I believe that there is now an urgent necessity for entering higher realms with our consciousness because of the impending changes on the planet. Through these higher realms, new healing energies and insights can be brought down to assist us in these coming Earth changes."
— David K. Miller

$16.95 • 176 PP. • Softcover • 978-1-891824-82-1

Biorelativity: Planetary Healing Technologies

Biorelativity describes the ability of human beings to telepathically communicate with the spirit of Earth. The goal of such communication is to influence the outcome of natural Earth events such as storms, volcanic eruptions, and earthquakes. Through the lessons contained in this book, you can implement new planetary healing techniques right now, actively participating in exciting changes as Earth and humanity come together in unity and healing.

$16.95 • 352 PP. • Softcover • 978-1-891824-98-2

A New Tree of Life for Planetary Ascension

This is the second book David Miller has written about the Kabbalah. His first book, Kaballah and the Ascension, introduced basic concepts in the Kabbalah and linked them to the ascended masters and the process of ascension. In this second book, David has teamed up with Torah scholar and Kabbalist expert Mordechai Yashin, who resides in Jerusalem, Israel. This book is based on unique lectures and classes David and Mordechai gave over an eight-month period between 2012 and 2013. These lectures on Jewish and Hebraic lessons were held in open discussion groups and offer a truly unique perspective into the Kabbalistic Tree of Life and how it has been expanded.

$16.95 • 464 PP. • Softcover • 978-1-62233-012-6

Raising the Spiritual Light Quotient

The spiritual light quotient is a measurement of a person's ability to work with and understand spirituality. This concept is compared to the intelligence quotient (IQ). However, in reality, spiritual ability is not related to intelligence, and interestingly, unlike the IQ, one's spiritual light quotient can increase with age and experience.

$16.95 • 384 PP. • Softcover • 978-1-891824-89-0

Connecting with the Arcturians

Who is really out there? Where are we going? What are our choices? What has to be done to prepare for this event? This book explains all of these questions in a way that we can easily understand. It explains what our relationships are to known extraterrestrial groups and what they are doing to help Earth and her people in this crucial galactic moment in time.

$17.00 • 256 PP. • Softcover • 978-1-891824-94-4

New Spiritual Technology for the Fifth-Dimensional Earth

Earth is moving closer to the fifth dimension. New spiritual ideas and technologies are becoming available for rebalancing our world, including native ceremonies to connect to Earth healing energies and thought projections and thought communication with Earth.

$19.95 • 240 PP. • Softcover • 978-1-891824-79-1

BOOKS BY DAVID K. MILLER

Fifth-Dimensional Soul Psychology

"The basic essence of soul psychology rests with the idea that the soul is evolving and that part of this evolution is occurring through incarnations in the third dimension. Now, to even speak about the soul evolving is perhaps a controversial subject because we know that the soul is eternal. We know that the soul has been in existence for infinity, and we know that the soul is perfect. So why would the soul have to evolve?

The answer to this question is complex, and we may not be able to totally answer it using third-dimensional terminology. But it is an important question to answer, because the nature of soul evolution is inherently connected to your experiences in the third dimension. The soul, in completing its evolutionary journey, needs these experiences in the third dimension, and it needs to complete the lessons here."

—Vywamus

$16.95 • 288 PP. • Softcover • 978-1-62233-016-4

Teachings from the Sacred Triangle, Vol. 1

David's second book explains how the Arcturian energy melds with that of the White Brother-/Sisterhood and the ascended Native American masters to bring about planetary healing.

Topics include the Sacred Triangle energy and the sacred codes of ascension, how to create a bridge to the fifth dimension, what role you can play in the Sacred Triangle, and how sacred words from the Kaballah can assist you in your ascension work.

$16.95 • 288 PP. • Softcover • 978-1-62233-007-2

Teachings from the Sacred Triangle, Vol. 2

Our planet is at a dire crossroads from a physical standpoint, but from a spiritual standpoint, it is experiencing a great awakening. Never before have there been so many conscious lightworkers, awakened spiritual beings, and masters as there are on this planet now. A great sense of a spiritual harmony emanates from the many starseed groups, and there is also a new spiritual energy and force that is spreading throughout the planet.

$16.95 • 288 PP. • Softcover • 978-1-891824-19-7

Teachings from the Sacred Triangle, Vol. 3

Learn how to use holographic technology to project energies in the most direct and transformative way throughout Earth.

Chapters Include:
- Heart Chakra and the Energy of Love
- Multidimensional Crystal Healing Energy
- Healing Space-Time Rifts
- Integration of Spirituality and Technology, Space, and Time Travel

$16.95 • 288 PP. • Softcover • 978-1-891824-23-4

Enseñanzas del Sagrado Triángulo Arcturiano

Este paradigma es necesario para ayudar en la transición de la humanidad hacia la próxima etapa evolutiva. La humanidad debe realizar esta próxima etapa de la evolución, para asegurar su sobrevivencia por los cambios climáticos globales, la guerra y la destrucción del medio ambiente. ¿Cuál es la próxima etapa? Esta involucra la expansión de la consciencia del ser humano y está representada por el símbolo de este nuevo paradigma, el Sagrado Triángulo Arcturiano.

El guía de la quinta dimensión, Juliano, proveniente del sistema estelar galáctico conocido como Arcturus, trabaja junto a David en un papel prominente en esta introducción de la energía del Triángulo Sagrado en la Tierra. David le ofrece al lector un entendimiento del alma, su naturaleza evolutiva y como la humanidad esta avanzando hacia esa siguiente etapa evolutiva.

$19.95 • 416 PP. • Softcover • 978-1-62233-264-9

Expand Your Consciousness

Now more than ever, humankind is in need of developing its higher consciousness to heal itself and Earth and to experience life in a much more meaningful way. By expanding our consciousness, we can see the connections and unity that exist in all reality, and we might see objects with sharper colors, hear sounds with greater clarity, or even experience two sensations simultaneously! In this book, you will explore the fascinating multidimensionality that is yours for the taking.

$16.95 • 288 PP. • Softcover • 978-1-62233-036-2

Sarah Goddard Neves

12 Steps TO A Lightness OF Being

This unique book has been designed as if you were taking a very special spiritual development course in the comfort of your own home. Through its wisdom and guided meditations — **included on the enclosed CDs to boost empowerment** — *12 Steps to a Lightness of Being* will gradually but surely lift your vibration and awaken you. Therefore, to get the most out of it, decide now not to rush it but to read it slowly. Take as long as you need on each step before moving on to the next. Commit to doing each meditation or visualization, giving yourself some quiet, undisturbed time to do this, and recall your meditation experiences and insights afterward. By doing so, you will get the most out of reading this book.

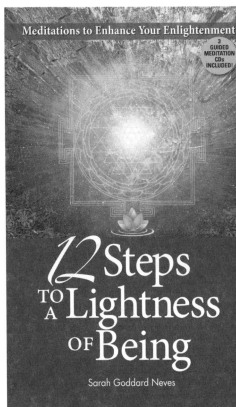

Meditations to Enhance Your Enlightenment

3 GUIDED MEDITATION CDs INCLUDED!

12 Steps TO A Lightness OF Being

Sarah Goddard Neves

$19.95 • Softcover • 160 PP.
6 X 9 • Perfect Bound
ISBN 978-1-891824-99-9

3 GUIDED MEDITATION CDs INCLUDED!

The Twelve Steps:

1. Meditation on the Light
2. Opening to Your Intuition
3. Master Connection
4. Being Happy
5. The Healing Power of Forgiveness
6. Evolving with Love and Light
7. Realizing Your Life's Purpose
8. Awakening to Love
9. You: a Creation and a Creator
10. Soul Reflection
11. Hope from the Stars
12. Becoming a Lightness of Being

HANDBOOK FOR HEALERS

by Frankie Z Avery & the OMA Group

Includes CD & DVD

OMA AND HEALING BOOK 1

HANDBOOK
FOR
HEALERS

Guidelines for a Wellness Practice

Frankie Z Avery & the OMA Group

Accompanied by an instructional DVD and a healing tones CD, the *Handbook for Healers* is intended for healers of all skill levels. OMA, channeled through Frankie Z Avery, offers advice on such issues as nutrition, lifestyle, and healing techniques. The companion DVD contains demonstrations of each of the meditations and exercises included. The *Healing Room Tones* CD is a creation of unique frequencies meant to enhance balance, harmony, and depth of perception in the healing room.

$25⁰⁰
Plus Shipping

ISBN 978-1-891824-72-2
Softcover • 192 PP.
6 x 9 Perfect Bound

CHAPTERS
- *What Distinguishes Healers*
- *What Healers Do*
- *How Healing Works*
- *The Healer*
- *The Healer with a Patient*
- *Optimized Healing Environments*
- *Happiness*
- *The Importance of Eating Well*

EXERCISES
- *Energize Your Day*
- *Check for Balance*
- *Expand Energy before Session*
- *Focus*
- *Balance with the Patient*
- *Stroke and Seal*
- *Cleanse between Patients*
- *Dust Off after Healing*
- *Restore: Catch Your Breath*
- *Breathe to Lighten Pain*